FROM PEN TO PEACE:

INTEGRATING WRITING AND REIKI FOR TRANSFORMATION

Nayanda M. Moore

This book is dedicated to my first teachers:

My mom, Pat, who always encouraged me to write and create, and Jeffrey Ratner, my 5th grade teacher and mentor.

May you both rest in eternal peace.

Write Your Life Journals Publishing®

———

First Edition: September 2024

———

ISBN 979-8-9914399-0-9 (eBook)
ISBN 979-8-9914399-1-6 (Paperback)
Write Your Life Journals Publishing
Book Size 5.5 x 8.5
Printed in the United States of America

"…given time and a piece of paper,
stress is literally taken from your mind
and made tangible."
Ty M.

TABLE OF CONTENTS

TABLE OF CONTENTS
(CONT'D)

TABLE OF CONTENTS
(CONT'D)

TABLE OF CONTENTS
(CONT'D)

TABLE OF CONTENTS
(CONT'D)

Table of Contents
(Cont'd)

TABLE OF CONTENTS
(CONT'D)

INTRODUCTION

Welcome to a transformative journey where the power of words meets the healing energy of Reiki. For the past decade, I have taught writing at the college level in New York City. My passion for the written word is matched only by my dedication to Reiki, a practice I have embraced as a Master Practitioner for over seven years.

Throughout my years of teaching, I've witnessed firsthand the therapeutic effects that writing can have on individuals, empowering them to release, reflect, and transform. This book is born from my dual experiences—as an educator helping students find their voice through writing, and as a healer facilitating personal growth and well-being through Reiki. It is my belief that writing, much like Reiki, is not merely a skill but a wonderful tool for healing and self-discovery.

In my approach, integrating Reiki into the classroom is essential. It begins with ensuring that I am centered, present, and attuned to students' needs before entering the classroom.

Setting a positive atmosphere for myself and my students is crucial to creating a safe and conducive environment for sharing. Each student is individually greeted and listened to attentively, fostering a supportive environment, especially when discussing challenging topics. Whether online or in-person, I welcome a warm, safe atmosphere into the classroom. Since I recognize music as the language of feelings, I incorporate it before and during introspective writing sessions. I've witnessed firsthand the transformative impact of this practice. Guiding students to document their thoughts, dreams, and aspirations has yielded remarkable results. Their voices and experiences, shared throughout this book, illuminate the influence of writing on shaping these realities.

As my Reiki practice has evolved, so has my approach with clients. I guide them to actively participate in their healing process, directing their intention and focus during sessions. I believe in the body's innate ability to heal itself. Through mutual commitment, greater outcomes can be achieved. While

I don't view myself as a traditional healer, I take pride in helping others find clarity and peace through our interactions.

The purpose of this book is to guide you in integrating these powerful practices into your own life. Whether you are an experienced writer seeking deeper personal engagement with your craft or new to using writing and Reiki for self-exploration, this book offers insights and exercises to enrich both your creative and healing journeys.

Each chapter serves as a steppingstone, building upon the previous one to deepen your understanding and practice of writing and Reiki. From exploring narrative construction basics to delving into the energy centers or chakras, you will learn to harness the transformative power of both words and energy for personal and spiritual growth.

Join me at Write-Your-Life.com as we embark on this path together, discovering how the collaborative synergy between writing and Reiki can enrich your life, heal your mind, and nourish your soul. Here's to beginning a journey of creativity, healing, and transformation!

"[I wrote] my story and it helped me heal."
Mariama K.

CHAPTER I.

THE POWER OF WRITING

Welcome to the first step of your journey where writing isn't just an act of communication, but a sincere means of transformation. In this chapter, we'll explore how writing can serve as a powerful tool for self-discovery, healing, and personal growth.

A.   The Therapeutic Benefits of Writing

1.   Expression of Self

Writing provides a unique space for expressing the self. It allows for the articulation of thoughts and emotions that might be difficult to verbalize, offering a form of therapy that is accessible at any time.

This is writing in your truth.

I grew up when children were seen, not heard. On paper, I heard my voice loud and clear. I could say words on paper I would never utter aloud to my parents. I discovered that expressing myself on paper validated my feelings when no one else could or would.

5

2.   Clarification of Thought

The act of writing encourages clearer thinking. It compels the writer to organize thoughts, which can lead to new insights and perspectives on personal issues.

Thoughts often arrive in disarray. I've learned that every idea or thought, once written down, can be actualized with focused attention. Putting them on paper helps me discern a clear direction or path forward.

3.   Stress Reduction

Regular writing can significantly reduce stress by managing and releasing negative thoughts and emotions. It is a well-known fact that journaling is linked to improved mental health outcomes.

There are moments when adhering to the Reiki tenet 'I will not be angry' feels impossible. During such times, I turn to a specific journal reserved for expressing my anger, knowing that voicing it aloud would be disruptive. I believe that pent-up emotions can manifest as physical ailments. Pouring out feelings of anger, disgust, or outrage into this dedicated notebook allows me to release them without dwelling on them further. I advocate for writing them down and letting them go without revisiting them. Through practice, you may find that the need for this type of "anger releasing" journal diminishes over time.

4.   Enhancing Self-Awareness

Writing not only reflects where you are in your emotional and spiritual journey but also helps chart the path for where you want to go. It fosters a greater understanding of oneself and one's motivations.

Writing has been instrumental in helping me understand my motivations, patterns, and their outcomes. By articulating why I took certain actions, I gained clarity and the ability to shift my perspective. Seeing my thoughts and behaviors in black and white allowed me to confront aspects of myself that I might not have liked—and empowered me to make changes. As I evolved, so did my choices.

"[I] believe in my identity as a writer."
Katrina M.

B. Scientific Insights and Expert Opinions

Therapeutic writing, especially expressive writing, has been extensively researched and is found to have significant benefits for mental and physical health. Key studies and findings that support the benefits of therapeutic writing are:

1. James Pennebaker and Expressive Writing

One of the most influential researchers in this area is James Pennebaker, who has conducted multiple studies on the benefits of expressive writing. His research found that writing about emotionally traumatic experiences for just 20 minutes over four consecutive days can lead to improvements in psychological health and even immune function. Participants in his studies often experienced better mood levels, reduced stress symptoms, and fewer illnesses.

2. Improvements in Physical Health

A study by Joshua Smyth et al. examined the impact of expressive writing on people with chronic diseases. The findings suggested that expressive writing resulted in significant reductions in disease symptoms and was particularly effective in improving lung function in asthma and rheumatoid arthritis conditions.

3. Mental Health Benefits

A systematic review by Karen Baikie and Kay Wilhelm demonstrated that expressive writing causes significant improvements in various mental health outcomes, including reduced stress and anxiety, fewer depressive symptoms, and improved mood.

4. Enhancing Cognitive Functioning

Research by Laura King showed that writing about achieving future goals and best possible selves could lead to an increased sense of well-being and improved health. This kind of writing helps individuals clarify their goals and reinforce their sense of identity and direction.

5.   Impact on Social Relationships

Studies suggest that expressive writing can also affect social relationships, leading to greater social engagement and higher quality of personal relationships, possibly because individuals process their emotions more effectively and communicate better.

A Personal Story

Growing up amidst the dysfunctional chaos of my family, I often found myself questioning the purpose of existence from a young age. I distinctly recall asking an adult, "Why are we born?" The silence that followed left an indelible impression on me; though I can't recall who I asked, the unanswered question lingered.

Observing the tumultuous lives around me, I struggled to reconcile the notion that life might simply be about enduring hardship before fading away. It didn't make sense to my young mind; there had to be something more, something meaningful. I began to envision what my adult self would need to feel fulfilled. Always questioning, I distilled my aspirations into a simple list:

- a career that I love
- a close, loving, and fun relationship with my children
- a partner who loves me as much as I love him

I envisioned the kind of life I wanted to lead as an adult. Yet, as life unfolded, dreams often stalled amid challenges. It wasn't until 2017 that I realized something significant: I was living the life I once envisioned.

Journaling proved invaluable during my young life, providing clarity and solace. Beyond its therapeutic benefits, I became an advocate for the power of writing down one's aspirations. It transforms dreams into tangible goals, granting permission to want what one truly desires.

C. <u>Writing Exercises</u>

1. Journal Writing

Start a nightly journal habit where you reflect on the day, noting any significant thoughts, feelings, and insights. Notice any patterns in your writing and acknowledge them.

2. Letter to Self

Write a letter to yourself with clear intentions on why you're writing. For example, you can write to your younger self to validate feelings or thoughts that may have been ignored.

3. Stream of Consciousness Writing

When you first wake up, write what comes into your awareness for the first 15 minutes. Thirty minutes if you can. Use a timer and when you're done, go about your day. At the end of the week, see if you notice any similarities of ideas or questions that come up in your writing.

We use writing not only to communicate with others but also to explore and understand ourselves. Writing is inherently about self-discovery. Scholars widely recognize that therapeutic writing can foster balanced and resilient lives through the introspection it demands.

I challenge you to incorporate one of these practices into your daily routine. For me, morning stream-of-consciousness writing has evolved into a spiritual practice. It serves as a ritual to align my body, mind, and spirit before I embark on my day's journey. In the next chapter, I will introduce the basics and benefits of Reiki practice.

"I never knew I had the ability to write so diligently . . .
it will forever be a cherished tool of mine."
Elizabeth B.

CHAPTER II.

INTRODUCTION TO REIKI

A.   <u>My Reiki Journey</u>

Practicing Reiki has deeply balanced my life, awakening a strong sense of gratitude and appreciation for the beauty that surrounds me daily. During my morning walks, I find myself marveling at the intricate formations of clouds, listening intently to the gentle whispers of the leaves, and feeling immense gratitude for the soothing caress of the wind. These moments have become anchors of peace and mindfulness, grounding me in the present moment and nurturing a meaningful connection with nature.

Moreover, my Reiki practice has illuminated my strengths and gifts, revealing them as tools to assist others on their own journeys. This awareness has not only deepened my sense of purpose but also empowered me to cultivate deeper, more meaningful friendships and relationships. Through Reiki, I've learned to approach challenges, such as the stresses of the pandemic, with resilience and clarity. Instead of succumbing to anxiety, I now ask myself, "What am I meant to learn from this experience?" or "How can I emerge stronger and more compassionate?"

In essence, practicing Reiki has brought me inner peace and serenity while also enriching my life with a deep appreciation for the interconnectedness of all beings, and the transformative power of compassion and self-awareness.

Reiki is an ancient healing practice that has gained widespread recognition for its ability to promote healing, reduce stress, and restore balance. Whether you are new to Reiki or looking to deepen your understanding, this chapter will provide you with foundational knowledge and practical insights.

B.   What is Reiki?

1.   Origins and History

Reiki is a form of energy healing that originated in Japan in the early 20th century. It was developed by Dr. Mikao Usui after a profound spiritual experience on Mount Kurama.

Dr. Usui dedicated his life to studying ancient healing techniques, leading to the development of Reiki as a systematized method of channeling universal life energy to promote healing.

2.   Principles of Reiki

Reiki is guided by five key principles, which serve as spiritual and ethical guidelines for practitioners. These principles emphasize personal and spiritual well-being and are often recited daily by Reiki practitioners as a form of meditation. The principles are:

1.   Just for today, I will not be angry.
2.   Just for today, I will not worry.
3.   Just for today, I will be grateful.
4.   Just for today, I will do my work honestly.
5.   Just for today, I will be kind to every living thing.

These principles encourage living in the present and promote a peaceful and mindful approach to life's challenges.

C.   The Reiki Practice

Reiki practice involves the practitioner placing their hands on or just above the body in various positions, often using specific symbols and intents to guide and modulate energy flow. This process is believed to stimulate the body's natural healing abilities and restore physical and emotional well-being.

Here is a breakdown of key concepts in Reiki practice:

1.   Energy Centers or Chakras[1]

Reiki is based on the belief that life energy flows through us, and disruptions in this energy flow can lead to physical and emotional imbalances. The practice focuses on the chakras or energy centers within the body that correspond to specific physical, emotional, and spiritual functions.

2.   Role of a Reiki Practitioner

A Reiki practitioner is trained to sense and manipulate the flow of energy through these centers. They use their hands

---

[1]   For this text, "chakras" and "energy centers" are used interchangeably. In medical environments, the term "energy centers" is preferred.

to transmit energy to the patient, facilitating healing by clearing blockages and balancing the body's energy systems.

3.   Levels of Reiki

There are typically three levels or degrees of Reiki training, each deepening the practitioner's ability to channel energy:

(a)   *First Degree*

Focuses on opening the energy channels to allow the practitioner to channel Reiki to themselves and others.

(b)   *Second Degree*

Includes the use of Reiki symbols and the ability to perform distant or absentee healing.

(c)   *Master Level*

The practitioner learns advanced techniques and receives the ability to teach and initiate others into Reiki.

The following chart details the main energy centers, the glands they are associated with, and their locations in the body.

CHAKRA	ASSOCIATED GLANDS	LOCATION IN BODY
Crown	Pineal	Top of the head
Third Eye	Pituitary	Center of the forehead, just above the eyebrows
Throat	Thyroid	Base of the throat
Heart	Thymus	Center of the chest, just above the heart
Solar Plexus	Adrenal	Upper abdomen, in the stomach area
Sacral	Reproductive	Lower abdomen, about two inches below the navel
Root	Reproductive	Base of spine, pelvic floor, and first 3 vertebrae

This chart provides a clear overview of how each energy center corresponds to specific glands and body locations, which can be useful in understanding how Reiki can potentially impact physical health and emotional well-being.

D.   Basic Techniques and Preparations for Reiki

As you begin your journey with Reiki, preparation is essential in understanding and mastering basic techniques. This section will guide you through initial practices that you can use to harmonize and enhance your energy flow, preparing you for deeper Reiki practice.

E. Preparing Yourself and Your Environment

1. Creating a Conducive Space

The environment in which you practice Reiki should promote a sense of calm and cleanliness. This might involve setting up a quiet area with minimal distractions, using elements such as soft lighting, comfortable seating, and soothing background music or natural sounds.

2. Mental and Physical Preparation

Prior to practicing Reiki, it's important to ensure that your mind and body are relaxed. Techniques such as deep breathing, meditation, or a few minutes of gentle yoga can help center your thoughts and loosen your body.

3. Setting Intentions

Before beginning a Reiki session, set a clear intention or goal for what you wish to achieve. This could be general, like achieving relaxation, or specific, like alleviating headache pain. Intentions help focus the energy and enhance the effectiveness of the practice.

F.   Basic Reiki Techniques

1.   Self-Reiki Hand Positions

Learn basic hand placements to administer Reiki to yourself. These positions correspond to the body's major chakras as indicated in the chart earlier in the chapter.

2.   Feeling the Energy

Beginners may initially struggle to sense energy. Practice feeling energy by rubbing your hands together vigorously for a few seconds, then pulling them apart slightly. Many people feel warmth, tingling, or pulsing—these are indications of energetic presence.

3.   Administering Reiki

Once you've prepared and sensed the energy, you can begin. Place your hands gently over or on the desired area and allow the energy to flow. There's no need to apply physical pressure—Reiki energy travels through and to where it's needed.

G.   Integrating Daily Reiki Practice

1.   Routine Practice

Incorporate Reiki into your daily routine. A daily session of even just 15 minutes can provide significant benefits, from reduced stress to improved focus and energy levels.

2.   Journaling Your Experience

Keep a Reiki journal to track your experiences, feelings, and any changes or insights you gain. This can be especially insightful as you progress in your practice.

These basic techniques and preparations are just the beginning of your Reiki journey. As you grow more comfortable with these practices, you will find that your ability to manage and direct energy improves, enhancing both your personal well-being and your effectiveness in using Reiki. Practice these techniques regularly with patience and persistence. Reiki is a skill that sharpens and becomes more impactful with practice and dedication.

The idea of using the hands to heal is not unique to Reiki practice. The following are other examples of a hands-on approach to health and well-being.

Examples of Hands-on Healing Practices

- **Ayurvedic Marma Therapy (India)**:
  In Ayurveda, an ancient Indian medical system, Marma points are considered vital areas of the body where flesh, veins, arteries, tendons, bones, and joints meet. Practitioners use their hands to massage these points gently to stimulate prana (life force) for therapeutic effects and to promote healing and balance within the body.

- **Jin Shin Jyutsu (Japan)**:
  This is a traditional Japanese healing art that involves gentle touch to balance the body's energy pathways. Practitioners use their hands to hold specific combinations of points on the body, which correspond to different energy pathways that can be blocked due to stress or illness.

- **Reflexology (Global)**:
  Reflexology involves applying pressure to specific points on the feet, hands, or ears. These points are believed to correspond to different

body organs and systems. Reflexology is used to promote health and well-being by stimulating these points and improving energy flow throughout the body.

- **Hawaiian Lomi Massage (Hawaii)**:
This traditional Hawaiian massage uses a combination of prayer, breathing, and intuitive movement with the hands to promote relaxation, healing, and spiritual connection. The therapists often use long, flowing motions that mimic the movement of waves over the body.

- **Qigong Healing (China)**:
Qigong is a holistic system of coordinated body posture, movement, breathing, and meditation used for health, spirituality, and martial arts training. In Qigong healing, practitioners may use their hands to direct or manipulate the flow of Qi (energy) in another person's body to aid in healing and balance.

- **Reconnective Healing (Modern/Western)**:
Developed by Dr. Eric Pearl, Reconnective Healing is a form of energy healing that is said to reconnect the lines of energy in our bodies and around the earth. Practitioners use their hands to sense and manipulate these energies, often without physical touch, to promote healing.

- **Christian Faith Healing (Global)**:
  In Christian traditions, the laying on of hands is practiced as part of prayer for divine healing. This practice involves everyone placing their hands on the sick person while prayers are said, invoking God's healing power.

Having experienced the power of Christian prayer circles, I've found that my Reiki practice not only aligns beautifully with my faith but also allows me to practice with people of different faiths without judgment.

H. Benefits of Reiki

1. Physical Health

(a) *Pain Management*

Reiki is widely recognized for its ability to reduce physical pain from ailments such as arthritis, sciatica, and migraines. It helps by promoting relaxation and reducing muscle tension and inflammation.

(b) *Enhanced Recovery*

Reiki can accelerate the body's natural healing processes, making it an excellent complementary therapy for post-operative recovery or chronic illness.

(c)   *Improved Sleep*

The calming effect of Reiki can help alleviate insomnia and improve the quality of sleep, leading to better overall health and vitality.

2.   Emotional and Mental Well-being

(a)   *Stress Reduction*

One of the most immediate benefits of Reiki is its ability to induce deep relaxation, which helps decrease stress and anxiety levels. This relaxation response can also help mitigate other mental health issues such as depression.

(b)   *Emotional Clarity and Peace*

Reiki can aid in the release of emotional baggage, leading to clearer and more positive thinking. It can also enhance one's ability to cope with frustrations and interpersonal conflicts.

(c)   *Enhancement of Mood*

Regular Reiki sessions can contribute to an overall sense of well-being and happiness, often attributed to the balancing of energy.

3. Spiritual Growth

(a)   *Increased Self-Awareness*

Reiki encourages introspection and mindfulness, which can lead to a deeper understanding of oneself and one's place in the universe.

(b)   *Spiritual Enlightenment*

For those on a spiritual path, Reiki can open and clear the chakras or energy centers, promoting a deeper spiritual connection and facilitating personal growth.

(c)   *Harmony and Balance*

Reiki teaches the body to reach an equilibrium where the body, mind, and spirit are in harmony, enhancing overall quality of life.

4. Additional Benefits

(a)   *Enhanced Creativity*

As Reiki clears mental clutter and balances emotions, it can open new avenues for creative thought and expression—beneficial for writers, artists, and any creative professionals.

(b)   *Improved Relationships*

By fostering empathy and clearer communication, Reiki can enhance personal relationships. Practice encourages compassion and understanding both towards oneself and others.

(c)   *Boosted Energy Levels*

Many people report feeling rejuvenated and energized after a Reiki session. This increased energy can enhance productivity and enjoyment of daily activities.

Here are some studies that have documented diverse benefits of Reiki:

(1)   Stress Reduction and Relaxation

A study conducted by Jane Van der Zee et al. in 2019 found that Reiki significantly reduced stress and anxiety in hospital patients compared to those who did not receive Reiki. The study suggests that Reiki could be an effective intervention for hospital environments to improve patient well-being.

(2)   <u>Pain Management</u>

A 2010 study by Karin Olson found that Reiki treatments significantly reduced pain in patients suffering from various chronic illnesses, including cancer and neurological disorders. The study underscores Reiki's potential as a complementary therapy in pain management strategies.

(3)   <u>Improvement in Sleep and General Well-being</u>

A randomized controlled trial by Vitale and O'Connor in 2006 examined the impact of Reiki on sleep patterns and general well-being in older adults. The findings indicated that participants who received Reiki experienced better sleep quality and greater overall well-being compared to a control group.

(4)   <u>Impact on Physiological Parameters</u>

Research by Baldwin and Schwartz in 2006 explored how Reiki could affect the autonomic nervous system. Their study demonstrated that Reiki increased the heart rate variability of participants, an indicator of reduced stress and enhanced resilience to stress.

(5)   <u>Enhancing Quality of Life for Cancer Patients</u>

A study by Dressen and Singg in 1998 focused
on cancer patients undergoing Reiki sessions
and found improvements in quality of life,
including reduced anxiety and improved mood
states, highlighting Reiki's potential as a
supportive therapy in oncology settings.

These studies provide scientific backing for the benefits
of Reiki across various aspects of physical and mental health,
making Reiki a credible and beneficial complementary therapy.

I.   <u>Concluding Thoughts on Reiki's Benefits</u>

As we've explored the various benefits of Reiki, it's
important to note that in my practice, I employ a hands-on
approach during one-on-one sessions. This method has been
highly effective as a complementary treatment alongside
traditional medicine, providing a holistic option that enhances
the healing process without interfering with medical
treatments.

Additionally, I administer Reiki distantly with similar
results. **Distance Reiki** is a practice where the Reiki
practitioner and client do not need to be physically present with

31

each other. This is possible because Reiki energy transcends physical distance and is directed by intention. During a distance Reiki session, practitioners use specific symbols and visualization techniques to connect to their clients and send healing energy across any distance, whether the client is in a different room or across the globe.

My clients, who have experienced both in-person and distance Reiki, attest to its effectiveness.

> "I am a newcomer to Reiki…my first distance treatment. The treatment left me feeling "lighter" and more centered in the days following."
> ~ *Laura P., Denver, Colorado* ~

> "…my sister had several Reiki sessions…which included "cleansing" the house. I am at a loss for how to describe what transpired during those sessions, but I can tell you that my sister, after three years of spiraling, finally regained the "light" in her voice, her smile, her eyes, her home, her everything that I had known years prior."
> ~ *Vaughn N., British Columbia, Canada* ~

"I feel elevated emotionally, spiritually and mentally after each encounter."
~ *Monica H., New York, New York* ~

"Her touch makes you feel as though you are being held, whatever emotions come up, whatever clearing has to be done, you feel safe to release it."
~ *Marlene N., Los Angeles, California* ~

By incorporating Reiki into your wellness routine—whether in-person or through distance sessions—you can access a versatile and insightful tool for healing and personal growth that complements and enhances traditional medical care.

In the next chapter we'll explore how integrating writing and Reiki can create a powerful synergy for personal growth, healing, and creative expression.

CHAPTER III.

INTEGRATING WRITING AND REIKI

In this section, we explore how the complementary practices of writing and Reiki can enhance each other, providing an integrated approach to self-improvement and wellness. By integrating these practices, individuals can deepen their understanding of themselves, unlock new levels of creativity, and achieve greater emotional and spiritual balance.

A. **Enhance Creativity Through Reiki**

1. **Energy Clearing for Creative Blocks**

Reiki can be used to clear energy blockages that might stifle creativity. Position your hands lightly touching or slightly above the sacral chakra, which is in the lower belly, just below the navel as it is associated with creative and sexual energy.

2. **Meditative Writing Following Reiki**

Incorporate the practice of meditative writing immediately following a Reiki session. Reiki can induce a deeply relaxed state, making it easier to access subconscious thoughts and ideas that can fuel creative writing.

B.   <u>Manage Writing Challenges with Reiki</u>

    1.   **Overcome Writer's Block**

Reiki can help dissolve the anxiety and stress that often contribute to writer's block. See the step-by-step guide for a self-Reiki session focusing on the third eye and throat energy centers at Paragraph E in this chapter.

    2.   **Sustain Writing Motivation**

Regular Reiki practice can improve overall energy levels and mental clarity, helping writers maintain their motivation and productivity over longer periods.

C.   <u>Post-Writing Reiki Sessions</u>

    1.   **Emotional Processing**

After intense writing sessions that may bring up emotional content, Reiki can be a valuable tool for processing and integrating these emotions. To activate the Reiki energy, place your hands at your heart center. Set your intention to release the emotion allowing it to dissolve on your exhale. You could say upon exhale, "I release the (insert emotion)" and upon inhale, "I welcome (insert emotion)."

Example: On the inhale say to yourself, "I welcome peace and clarity." On the exhale say, "I release fear and confusion."

2. Physical Relief

Writing for extended periods of time can lead to physical discomfort, particularly in the neck, back, and shoulders. Reiki positions that specifically target these areas to relieve tension and prevent strain are located at Paragraph F in this chapter.

D. Create a Routine

1. Daily Rituals

Start a daily routine that incorporates both writing and Reiki. For example, start the day with a short Reiki session to energize and clear the mind, followed by a writing Session. Conclude with Reiki to unwind and process.

2. Writing and Reiki Journal

Keep a combined journal to document both Reiki experiences and writing insights. This can help track progress, patterns, and breakthroughs over time.

E. Self-Reiki Session for the Third Eye and Throat Chakras

1. Preparation

(a) *Find a Quiet Space*

Choose a quiet, comfortable space where you will not be disturbed. This can be a dedicated meditation area or any place that feels peaceful.

(b) *Set the Environment*

Optionally, you may want to play soft, calming music and dim the lights or light some candles to create a relaxing atmosphere.

(c) *Comfortable Position*

Sit or lie down in a comfortable position. Make sure your neck and back are supported so you can relax fully without holding any tension in your muscles.

2. Starting the Session

(a) *Grounding and Centering*

Begin by taking deep, slow breaths. Place hands at the first and second chakras. [Fig. 9] Inhale through your nose and exhale through your mouth.

37

With each breath, feel more relaxed and grounded. Allow your shoulders to fall away from your ears. Visualize roots growing from the soles of your feet deep into the earth, anchoring you firmly to the ground.

(b)   *Activate Reiki Energy*

Place your hands together in a prayer position near your heart. [Fig. 8] Close your eyes and express your intention to use Reiki for balancing and healing your third eye and throat chakras. You might say, "I invite this Reiki energy in to balance and heal my third eye and throat chakras for improved insight and communication."

3.   Reiki Hand Positions

(a)   *Third Eye Chakra (Ajna):*

(i)   Place your hands gently over your forehead, with fingertips touching the hairline. The third eye chakra is in the center of the forehead, just above the eyebrows. [Fig. 1]

(ii)   Hold this position and allow Reiki to flow into the third eye chakra. Imagine an indigo light (the color associated with the third eye chakra) emanating from your hands and penetrating the area, soothing, and balancing it.

(iii) Continue for about 3-5 minutes, focusing on the flow of energy and any sensations you might feel, such as warmth, tingling, or relaxation.

(b) *Throat Chakra (Vishuddha):*

(i) Move your hands to your throat, wrapping them gently around your neck or placing them flat against your throat chakra, which is located at the base of the neck. [Fig. 2]

(ii) Envision a bright blue light (the color associated with the throat chakra) flowing from your hands into your neck, clearing any blockages and promoting ease of expression.

(iii) Maintain this position for another 3-5 minutes, concentrating on any changes in your throat area,

39

feeling more openness and
clearer communication.

4. Closing the Session

(a) *Thank Your Practice*

Gently remove your hands from your
throat and place them back in the prayer
position near your heart. Thank yourself
and the Reiki energy for this healing
session. [Fig. 8]

(b) *Ground Yourself Again*

Take a few deep breaths, feeling the
ground beneath you. When you feel
ready, gently open your eyes, and move
slowly, bringing awareness back to your
surroundings.

(c) *Drink Water*

It's important to drink water after a Reiki
session to help flush out any toxins that
were released during the session.

(d) *Journaling*

Afterwards, you may want to write down
any insights, emotions, or thoughts that
arose during the session. This can be a
wonderful way to integrate the

experience into your writing and creative expression.

This simple self-Reiki session can be a powerful tool for writers, helping to clear mental blocks and enhance communication abilities. Practice regularly or whenever you feel the need for increased clarity and expressive power.

There are specific Reiki hand positions that can target the back, neck, and shoulders, which are areas that often accumulate tension from prolonged periods of writing. These positions can help relieve discomfort and promote relaxation.

F.   Reiki Hand Positions for Back, Neck, and Shoulders

1.   For the Back

(a)   *Lower Back*

(i)   Sit in a chair or on the floor or lie down comfortably. Place your hands on your lower back, covering the area just above the hips. This targets the sacral chakra, which is often associated with lower back issues. [Fig. 3]

(ii)   *Intend* for Reiki energy to flow into the lower back, soothing any

tension or pain. *Hold* this
position for 3-5 minutes.

(b)   *Middle Back*

(i)   Move your hands to the middle
of your back, just below the
ribcage. This can be more
accessible while sitting in a chair.
[Fig. 4]

(ii)   *Focus* the Reiki energy on
relaxing the muscles and easing
any stiffness. *Maintain* this
position for another 3-5 minutes.

(c)   *Upper Back*

(i)   For the upper back, which
impacts the area around the heart
chakra, place your hands on the
upper back, between the shoulder
blades. [Fig. 5]

(ii)   *Allow* the Reiki energy to
penetrate this area, promoting
relaxation and releasing tension.
Continue for 3-5 minutes.

2. For the Neck

(a) *Front of the Neck*

   (i) Gently place your hands at the base of your throat, covering the throat chakra. This position is beneficial for writers, as it helps enhance communication and self-expression. [Fig. 2]

   (ii) Keep your hands here for about 3-5 minutes, letting Reiki energy work to alleviate any tightness and enhance energy flow.

(b) *Back of the Neck*

   (i) Place one hand on the back of your neck, where the spine meets the skull. This area is crucial for relieving stress and tension headaches. [Fig. 6]

   (ii) *Hold* this position for 3-5 minutes, focusing on smoothing out any knots or tension.

3.   For the Shoulders

(a)   *Shoulder Tops*

(i)   Place each hand on a shoulder, gently covering the area where most people hold tension. [Fig. 7]

(ii)   *Direct* the Reiki energy to release this common stress storage point. Maintain this position for 3-5 minutes, imagining the stress melting away under your hands.

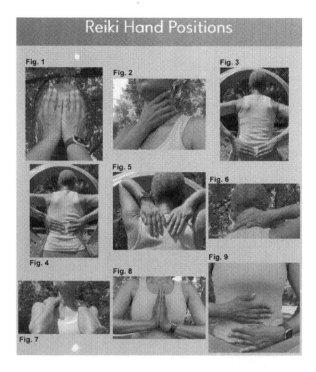

Reiki Hand Positions

Fig. 1   Fig. 2   Fig. 3

Fig. 5   Fig. 6

Fig. 4   Fig. 9

Fig. 8

Fig. 7

G. General Tips

1. Relaxation is Key

Ensure both you (the giver) and the recipient (if you're practicing on someone else) are comfortable and relaxed throughout the session.

2. Intention Matters

Always start with a clear intention of what you want to achieve with your Reiki session—whether it's pain relief, relaxation, or simply recharging your energy.

3. Consistent Practice

For best results, incorporate these Reiki sessions regularly into your routine, especially after extended periods of writing or desk work.

These Reiki positions can help writers and others who experience discomfort from sitting and focusing for lengthy periods. They provide a method to not only relieve physical tension but also to enhance overall well-being by balancing energy flow in the body. The time frame given is only a suggestion. Continue to hold the positions until you feel relief.

The combination of these practices is not just about improving writing or healing alone. It is also about fostering a more philosophical connection with one's inner self and enhancing the overall quality of life. I invite you to try incorporating these techniques to enhance your clarity and creativity.

CHAPTER IV.

DEVELOPING A PERSONAL PRACTICE

In developing your practice, both consistency and personalization are crucial to keep you engaged. Consistency builds and sustains the benefits of writing and Reiki, while personalization ensures the practice remains enjoyable and sustainable, seamlessly fitting into your daily life. Your invocation to draw energy may vary with each session. One day, you may use your Reiki practice to relieve tension, while another day, it may be focused on alleviating pain or stress.

A.   Assessing Your Needs and Goals

1.   Self-Assessment

Assess your current physical, emotional, and spiritual states. What are you hoping to achieve with your practice? Stress relief? Creative expression? Spiritual growth?

2.   Setting Clear Goals

It is important to set SMART (Specific, Measurable, Achievable, Relevant, Time-bound) goals for both your writing and Reiki practices. For example, commit to write for 30 minutes each morning or perform a 15-minute Reiki self-healing session before bedtime. Finding what works for you may take time but commit to the process.

B. **Creating a Personalized Schedule**

1. **Finding the Right Time**

Look at your schedule to determine the best times for your writing and Reiki practices. Morning might be best for writing when the mind is clear, while evenings could be ideal for Reiki to unwind and process the day. There is no wrong way to practice if it aligns with your schedule.

2. **Integrating Practices into Daily Life**

Use Reiki during breaks to recharge, during a warm bath to relax, or keep a journal handy for spontaneous writing sessions.

C. **Building a Conducive Environment**

1. **Physical Space**

Create a dedicated space for writing and Reiki. Surround yourself with things you love, colors that excite you, symbols that you revere. Find comfortable seating, beautiful pens, textured journals, inspirational objects, and affirmations that resonate with you. Invite these items to create a space you would enjoy spending time in.

2.   Ambience

It is also important to create the right ambience with elements like lighting, scents (e.g., essential oils), and background music that helps you to focus and relax.

D.   Developing Discipline and Flexibility

1.   Routine Building

It is easy to want to go all out and fully immerse yourself but please do not. Begin with shorter, more manageable sessions and gradually increase the duration as your practice becomes a habit. You want to build up your practice so you can see the results.

2.   Being Flexible

While routine is beneficial, flexibility is also crucial. Allow yourself some grace as you practice. Everyone must be adaptable to accommodate life's unpredictabilities.

E.   Enhancing Your Practice

1.   Continued Learning

If you are interested in studying Reiki on a deeper level,

workshops, books, and courses are available everywhere. My

recommendation for finding a Reiki practitioner is to learn how

they operate to see if it aligns with your core values. Every

practitioner is different, and it is imperative you find someone

who resonates with you. One trait you might look for is

someone who self-practices consistently.

2.   Community Engagement

There are benefits of joining writing groups and Reiki

circles to connect with like-minded individuals for support and

motivation.

Joining writing groups and Reiki circles offers a variety

of benefits that can significantly enhance both personal and

professional growth. These communities provide support,

learning opportunities, and a sense of belonging that can be

invaluable, especially when navigating the often solitary

practices of writing and Reiki. A detailed look at the benefits follows.

F.   Benefits of Joining Writing Groups

1.   Feedback and Critique

Members of writing groups regularly share their work and receive constructive feedback from peers. This process can dramatically improve writing skills, helping writers refine their style, fix structural issues, and develop their voice.

2.   Accountability

Regular meetings and deadlines can motivate members to write more consistently. Knowing that others expect to see your work can push you to finish projects and stick to a writing schedule.

3.   Inspiration and Ideas

Engaging with diverse writers exposes you to different perspectives and ideas that can spark your creativity. Discussions about writing techniques, themes, and character development can provide fresh insights and inspiration.

4.   **Networking**

Writing groups connect you with people who share your interests and goals. These connections can lead to collaborations, publishing opportunities, and friendships.

5.   **Support and Encouragement**

Writing can be an isolating activity. A writing group offers a supportive community that understands the challenges of the creative process and can provide encouragement during tough times.

"Writing is extremely liberating to me."
TM

G.   **Benefits of Joining Reiki Circles**

1.   **Shared Healing**

In Reiki circles, energy is multiplied and shared among participants, often resulting in more powerful healing experiences. Practicing in a group can enhance the individual's ability to direct energy and experience deeper healing.

2.   Learning and Growth

More experienced practitioners often lead or participate in Reiki circles, providing a valuable learning opportunity for less experienced members. Observing and discussing various techniques and experiences can broaden your understanding of Reiki.

3.   Community and Connection

Reiki circles offer a sense of community and belonging that can be particularly powerful for spiritual growth. They provide a safe and supportive environment to explore personal and spiritual issues.

4.   Consistent Practice

Regular meetings encourage consistent practice, which is crucial for developing and maintaining Reiki skills. The structured setting of a Reiki circle can help practitioners stay committed to their Reiki journey.

5.   Energy Attunement

Participating in Reiki circles can help practitioners maintain their energy attunement, keeping their abilities strong and their practice effective.

H.   Overall Benefits

Both writing groups and Reiki circles enhance personal discipline, offer social interaction, and provide emotional support. They allow for the exchange of knowledge and skills that can accelerate personal development and deepen practice in ways that might not be possible alone. For those looking to expand their skills and integrate into a community, these groups and circles are invaluable resources.

I.   Regular Reflection and Adaptation

1.   Journaling

Use a journal to reflect on the progress of both writing and Reiki practices. What works? What doesn't? How do the practices make you feel?

2.   Adjustments

If you find something is not working, make periodic adjustments to your practices based on your journal reflections and changing needs. Remember, change is the only constant. If we can navigate the changes in our lives, we can pivot our practices accordingly when life becomes chaotic.

Patience and persistence are key when integrating Reiki practice with your writing practice. Just know that developing a personal practice is a journey that evolves and deepens over time, offering great benefits along the way.

CHAPTER V.

SUSTAINING AND DEEPENING YOUR WRITING

AND REIKI PRACTICES

Becoming proficient in writing takes time and practice. Every writer continues to learn throughout their life. Enjoy the journey of discovering your unique voice and expressing your inner self through writing. Please review the Appendix and Resources lists in the back of this book.

A. <u>Sustaining Your Writing Practice</u>

1. Regular Writing Habits

(a) *Set Consistent Writing Time*

Establish a daily or weekly routine where you dedicate a specific time to write. Consistency helps turn writing into a habit.

(b) *Create Writing Rituals*

Incorporate small rituals, such as lighting a candle, playing specific music, or starting with a Reiki self-treatment to clear the mind and set intentions.

2. **Continued Learning**

   (a) *Read Widely and Often*

        Exposure to distinctive styles, genres, and authors can inspire and teach unfamiliar writing techniques.

   (b) *Take Workshops and Courses*

        Regularly participating in educational opportunities keeps skills sharp and introduces innovative writing concepts and tools.

3. **Join Writing Communities**

   (a) *Participate in Writing Groups and Workshops*

        These communities provide motivation, accountability, and valuable feedback. They also offer a chance to connect with like-minded individuals who can support and challenge you in your writing journey.

   (b) *Engage in Writing Challenges*

        Participate in challenges like NaNoWriMo (National Novel Writing Month) or writing prompts from sites like Reedsy.com to keep your writing fresh and exciting.

B.   Deepening Your Reiki Practice

1.   Regular Practice

(a)   *Daily Self-Reiki*

Incorporate Reiki into your daily routine. Start or end your day with a self-Reiki session. This not only maintains your connection to Reiki energy but also promotes personal well-being.

(b)   *Reiki on Others*

Offering Reiki to others, including pets, can deepen your understanding and proficiency. It provides insights into different energy experiences and enhances your intuitive abilities. Find a practitioner you resonate with if you want to pursue certification.

2.   Advanced Training

(a)   *Pursue Higher Degrees of Reiki*

Advanced Reiki training, such as achieving Reiki Master status, not only deepens your own practice but also allows you to teach and attune others, expanding the practice and your understanding of Reiki.

(b)   *Explore Integrative Techniques*

You can learn how to incorporate other healing modalities, such as crystal healing or aromatherapy with Reiki, to enrich your practice and offer more comprehensive healing sessions.

3.   Meditation and Mindfulness

(a)   *Integrate Meditation*

Regular meditation can enhance the connection to Reiki energy and improve the flow during healing sessions.

(b)   *Practice Mindfulness*

Mindfulness in daily life increases your sensitivity to energy in yourself and others, enhancing your Reiki practice.

C.   Integrating Both Practices

1.   Reflective Practices

(a)   *Journaling*

As noted in a prior section, maintaining a journal to reflect on your experiences and growth in both writing and Reiki can be a valuable tool for tracking progress, understanding personal shifts, and setting future goals.

2. Retreats and Sabbaticals

(a) *Attend or Create Retreats*

Participate in or organize retreats focused on writing and Reiki. Provide immersive experiences that can significantly deepen both practices.

(b) *Take Creative Sabbaticals*

Periodically dedicate time away from daily routines to focus intensely on writing and Reiki, allowing for deep reflection and significant advancement in skills.

Any practice requires a mindset of lifelong learning and curiosity. Both writing and Reiki are practices where there is always more to explore and understand. By embracing the journey and recognizing that each step is an opportunity for growth, practitioners can enjoy continual renewal and deepening of their skills.

D. Embarking on Your Journey

Combining the practices of writing and Reiki offers the following:

1. **A Holistic Approach**

Combining writing and Reiki offers a holistic approach to self-expression and healing, benefiting all aspects of one's life—mental, emotional, physical, and spiritual.

2. **Growth and Self-Discovery**

Writing and Reiki are not just skills to be learned, but pathways to personal growth and self-discovery. Each practice enriches the other, leading to deeper insights and greater well-being.

3. **Community and Support**

If community support is important, these practices have it. Whether you desire a writing group or a Reiki circle, connections with others provides support, inspiration, and opportunities for further learning.

E. **Ongoing Engagement**

Think of this book not just as a resource, but as a beginning point for a deeper exploration into integrating your writing and Reiki practices.

1. Continued Learning

Remain curious and open to learning. Read different authors. Keep experimenting with different techniques and practices discussed and adapt them according to your personal growth and changing needs.

2. Invitation to Join my Website

I invite you to continue your discovery of writing and Reiki by heading to my website: Write-Your-Life.com. There you can find Reiki inspired prompts, learn more about future courses, retreats, and explore resources for all your writing needs. Whether you're writing to rid yourself of self-limiting beliefs or you have an idea for a story, Write-Your-Life.com will get you writing about what's important to you. Decide what YOU want to create in your life. Write-Your-Life.com is a judgment-free writing zone. Therefore, even if you have never written before, this site is for you.

F.   Practice and Integration

1.   Daily Writing Prompts

Daily or weekly prompts can encourage you to practice the techniques discussed. You can find several prompts to get you started at the end of this chapter.

2.   Reflective Writing

Practice Reiki before writing to clear the mind and enhance focus, then after, write to reflect on your session or any ideas that came to you during your self-practice.

3.   Combining Practices

A simple exercise that combines Reiki and writing includes meditating on a story idea during Reiki and then writing about the insights gained. Remember, your journey is just beginning. The practices of writing and Reiki are excellent tools for transformation and healing - not just for the self, but also for the world around you. I invite you to access my website, where you can dive deeper into these practices, supported by a community of like-minded individuals eager to grow and learn together. Let's continue this journey, exploring new depths of creativity and wellness. Visit Write-Your-Life.com to learn more. Your story, powered by the healing energy of Reiki, is just starting to unfold.

G. <u>Closing Thoughts</u>

Continue your journey in writing and Reiki. Include these spiritual practices in addition to others you may have to develop a deeper understanding of yourself and your purpose.

"[Writing] helped me figure out how my story can be relatable."
Kadeem L.

CHAPTER VI.

WRITING 101

The following information offers basic details on everything you need to draft your first story or begin integrating a writing and Reiki practice. Printable PDFs are available to download on Write-Your-Life.com.

A. **Writing Foundations to Get You Started**

    1. **Expand Narrative Skills**

        (a) *Sequential Storytelling*

        Build a story with a clear beginning, middle, and end. Add interest by varying the way you tell a story. For instance, you can begin with the ending, or tell the story from an adult or child perspective.

        (b) *Character Depth*

        Develop more complex characters by exploring their backgrounds, motivations, and conflicts. See the provided template for creating character profiles at Paragraph 6 of this chapter.

(c)   *Setting and Atmosphere*

Setting in storytelling sets the tone and mood for your narrative. Instead of naming a place, use descriptive language to enhance how the setting looks and feels, as described in Paragraph 5 of this chapter.

2.   Use Basic Literary Techniques

(a)   *Themes and Messages*

Many writers have themes and messages throughout their stories. Start with a message you want to convey and build your story around it.

(b)   *Basic Symbolism*

Symbolism can be as simple as using weather (rain for sadness, sunshine for happiness) or colors to represent emotions or themes. Using symbolism adds depth to your writing and engages your audience.

(c)   *Dialogue Basics*

When writing dialogue, we often write too much. Many people do not speak in full complete sentences. Before you begin writing dialogue, listen to how people speak in real life. How do people respond to questions? How different is the dialogue of friends or family from the dialogue of colleagues?

3. Editing Techniques

(a) *Self-Editing Strategies*

If you are writing, reading aloud to catch awkward phrasing is one of the best self-editing techniques I use. I notice inconsistencies and errors in tense and perspective easily when I read my work aloud. Also, do not be afraid to use spell-check and grammar tools. You do not have to agree with the suggestions; however, read it aloud to ensure the context is correct.

(b) *Feedback and Revisions*

You can share your work with friends or in writing groups to get feedback. Think of the revision process as re-seeing your work for an opportunity to improve and refine your writing.

(c) *Keeping Readers Engaged*

To keep your writing interesting for your readers, you must have a relevant story.

Challenge yourself by looking at your story through different perspectives. Chose which voice or lens through which to tell it. Include a mix of action, description and dialogue in active voice while varying sentence length.

4.   **Exercise: Structuring a Narrative**

(a)   *Objective*

Practice creating a cohesive narrative with a clear beginning, middle, and end.

(b)   *Instructions*

Write a short story of about 500 words. Start with an introduction to the setting and characters, move into a conflict or a pivotal moment, and conclude with a resolution. Focus on ensuring each part flows logically into the next.

5.   **Using the Descriptive Language List: Integration, Variety and Sensory Details**

Practice integrating these descriptors seamlessly into your writing. Use these words to enhance the vividness of your scenes without overloading sentences with adjectives. Remember to vary the use of descriptive language to keep the writing fresh and engaging. Use all five senses to create rich, immersive experiences for the reader.

(a) *Atmospheric Conditions*

- **Weather**: Misty, blustery, sweltering, crisp, torrential, drizzling, balmy

- **Light**: Glimmering, shadowy, dim, harsh, dusky, radiant, flickering

(b) *Textures and Surfaces*

- **Textures**: Rough, smooth, jagged, silky, leathery, gritty, velvety

- **Surfaces**: Polished, weathered, rugged, glassy, porous, speckled

(c) *Colors and Patterns*

- **Colors**: Vibrant, muted, pastel, neon, dusky, shimmering, faded

- **Patterns**: Striped, speckled, mottled, plaid, chevron, paisley, floral

(d) *Sounds*

- **Nature Sounds**: Rustling, chirping, roaring, babbling, howling, whistling, crunching

- **Urban Sounds**: Buzzing, clattering, beeping, humming, rattling, clanging, echoing

(e) *Scents and Tastes*

- **Scents**: Musty, acrid, fragrant, tangy, burnt, fresh, earthy

- **Tastes**: Bitter, sweet, tangy, savory, salty, rich, zesty

(f) *Emotions and Feelings*

- **Positive Emotions**: Jubilant, serene, elated, buoyant, content, blissful

- **Negative Emotions**: Sullen, distraught, irate, despondent, anxious, morose

(g) *Movements and Actions*

- **Slow Movements**: Creeping, lumbering, meandering, drifting, sauntering

- **Fast Movements**: Dashing, hurtling, catapulting, whisking, darting

(h) *Shapes and Sizes*

- **Shapes**: Circular, angular, tapered, spiral, irregular, symmetrical
- **Sizes**: Minuscule, colossal, sprawling, compact, towering, diminutive

6. Character Profile Template

This template not only aids in creating complex and believable characters but also serves as a tool for maintaining consistency in character portrayal throughout a piece of writing. It helps you to think deeply about your characters, making them more engaging and relatable to readers.

(a) *Basic Information*

(i) **Name**: Full name, including any nicknames or aliases.

(ii) **Age**: Current age and date of birth.

(iii) **Appearance**: Height, build, hair color, eye color, distinctive features (e.g., scars, tattoos).

(iv) **Occupation**: Current job and brief job history, relevance to the story.

(b) *Background*

(i) **Family**: Immediate family members, relationship status with each, and their influence on the character.

(ii) **Education**: Level of education, notable school experiences, and impact on their current life.

(iii) **Socioeconomic Status**: Economic background, current living conditions.

(iv) **Cultural Background**: Ethnicity, religion, and how these influence their worldview.

(c) *Personality Traits*

(i) **General Disposition**: Introvert or extrovert, optimistic or pessimistic, stable or volatile.

(ii) **Strengths**: Key positive traits (e.g., intelligence, compassion, resilient).

(iii) **Weaknesses**: Main flaws or areas of vulnerability (e.g., impulsiveness, jealous, insecure).

(iv) **Hobbies and Interests**: What they do in their leisure time and why.

(d) *Motivations and Goals*

(i) **Short-term Goals**: What they hope to achieve during the timeline of your story.

(ii) **Long-term Goals**: Their aspirations for the future beyond the story.

(iii) **Motivations**: Why they seek these goals—driving desires, needs, or fears.

(e) *Relationships*

(i) **Significant Others**: Details about past and present romantic relationships.

(ii)   **Friends**: Key friendships, how these relationships influence them.

(iii)   **Enemies**: Who opposes them and why? The nature of these adversarial relationships.

(f)   *Conflicts and Challenges*

    (i)   **Internal Conflicts**: Psychological struggles, fears, doubts, or ethical dilemmas they face.

    (ii)   **External Conflicts**: Challenges posed by the environment, other characters, or societal expectations.

(g)   *Development Arc*

    (i)   **Character Growth**: How they will change throughout the story.

    (ii)   **Challenges for Growth**: Specific events that will test them and facilitate their growth.

    (iii)   **Resolution**: How their internal and external conflicts resolve by the end of the story.

(h)   *Miscellaneous*

    (i)   **Secrets**: Things only the character (and perhaps the reader) knows.

    (ii)   **Quirks**: Unique habits or behaviors that make the character stand out.

    (iii)   **Fears**: Phobias or deep-seated fears that affect their behavior.

(i)   *Usage Notes*

Fill out as much of the template as relevant but remember, not all details need to appear directly in the story. Instead, this information can inform how you write the character's dialogue and actions.

Revisiting and updating the character profile as your story evolves or as new character details are developed during the writing process. Characters can change during the writing process so remain open.

7. Writing Prompts

Story Creation Prompts

Here are 10 writing prompts that can stimulate creativity and help writers practice crafting concise and engaging responses.

1. Unexpected Friend: Write a story about a day in the life of a stray cat who makes an unusual friend in a busy urban park.

2. Lost and Found: Describe a character's emotions and actions when they discover a lost letter from someone important in their past.

3. The Last Cup: Imagine a world where coffee has become a rare commodity. Write about a character enjoying what could be their last cup.

4. Midnight Call: Your character receives a mysterious phone call at midnight. Who is it from, and what do they want?

5.   <u>Colorful World</u>: Write a descriptive paragraph about a street market, focusing intensely on the colors and what they signify.

6.   <u>Secret Ingredient</u>: A family recipe has a secret ingredient with magical properties. What is it, and how does it affect those who eat it?

7.   <u>Mirror Image</u>: A character finds an old mirror in an attic that shows not the reflection, but their truest self. What do they see?

8.   <u>Forgotten Path</u>: Describe a journey on an old, forgotten path that leads your character to a surprising destination.

9.   <u>Weathered Pages</u>: A character finds an old, weathered book in their new apartment. What is its title, and why is it significant?

10.   Digital Detox: Your character decides to spend a day without any digital devices. Detail their experiences and discoveries throughout the day.

Prompts for Self-Discovery and Personal Growth

The following prompts are designed to be deeply reflective, helping writers to examine and articulate their personal journeys and growth. These prompts encourage introspection and exploration of one's inner self, experiences, and beliefs.

1.   Defining Moments: Write about a moment in your life that defined or changed you significantly. How did it shape who you are today?

2.   Letter to Your Younger Self: Compose a letter to your younger self. What advice would you give? What reassurances or warnings would you include?

3.	Future Vision: Imagine yourself five years from now. What does your life look like? Describe your achievements, lifestyle, and how you feel about your progress.

4.	Core Values: List your top five core values. Write about why they are important to you and how you live them out in your daily life.

5.	Overcoming Obstacles: Think of a significant obstacle or challenge you've overcome. Detail the journey and the strategies that helped you succeed.

6.	Gratitude List: Create a detailed list of things you are grateful for. Expand on a few items, explaining why they bring you joy or peace.

7.	The Unlived Life: Discuss aspects of your life you wish to explore or dreams you want to pursue. What has held you back, and how can you take steps toward these desires?

8. Inspirational People: Write about someone who has significantly influenced your life. Describe how they impacted you and which of their qualities you aspire to emulate.

9. Facing Fears: Identify a fear you have and explore its origins. Write about steps you could take to confront and possibly overcome this fear.

10. Reflection on Change: Reflect on how you have changed in the last year. What events or thoughts initiated these changes? How do you feel about this evolution?

Character Development Prompts

1.   The Secret Keeper: Create a character who is known for keeping secrets. Write a scene where they are forced to reveal one of their secrets to someone they trust.

2.   Crossroads Decision: Develop a character standing at a crucial crossroad in their life. Describe their thought process as they decide which path to take, highlighting their fears, hopes, and motivations.

Setting Descriptions Prompts

1.   Abandoned Place: Describe an abandoned house that your character stumbles upon. Focus on sensory details that evoke a strong atmosphere, such as the sound of creaking floorboards or the sight of peeling wallpaper.

2. City at Night: Write a detailed description of a bustling city at night through the eyes of a newcomer. Highlight the contrasts between the darkness and the city lights, and the mixture of noises.

Dialogue Prompts

1. Revelation in Conversation: Write a dialogue between two characters where one reveals a surprising piece of news to the other. Focus on their reactions and the dynamic changes in the conversation.

2. First Meeting: Craft a dialogue where two characters meet for the first time in an unusual situation. Ensure the dialogue reflects their personalities and the peculiarity of their meeting place.

8. **Exercise: Integrating Writing and Reiki**

(a)   *Objective*: Use Reiki to enhance creativity and depth in writing.

(b)   *Instructions*:

   (i)   Begin with a 10-minute Reiki session focusing on the third eye and crown chakras to enhance intuition and creativity.

   (ii)   Immediately after the session, write a reflective piece about the experience or continue a work in progress, noting any new insights or ideas that arise.

   (iii)   Reflect on how the Reiki session influenced the writing in terms of ideas, clarity, and emotional depth.

CHAPTER VII.

KEY TAKEAWAYS FROM THE CHAPTERS

1.   Introduction to Writing and Reiki

Interconnected Growth: Writing and Reiki are complementary practices that enhance self-expression and personal healing, fostering both creativity and emotional well-being.

2.   Foundational Techniques

Building Blocks: Basic techniques in writing (such as structure, character development, and dialogue) and Reiki (such as hand positions and energy sensing) are essential for establishing a solid foundation in both fields.

3.   Integrating Writing with Reiki

Enhanced Creativity and Healing: Combining writing and Reiki can deepen the healing and creative processes, with Reiki clearing mental and emotional blockages, and writing providing a therapeutic outlet for expression.

4.   **Developing a Personal Practice**

Customization and Consistency: Developing a personalized and consistent practice in both writing and Reiki is crucial for long-term success and satisfaction. This involves setting routines, creating conducive environments, and regularly reflecting on personal growth.

5.   **Advanced Techniques and Deepening Practice**

Continuous Learning and Community Engagement: Advanced techniques in both writing and Reiki offer pathways to further deepen skills and understanding. Participation in communities such as writing groups and Reiki circles provides support, inspiration, and opportunities for further growth.

6.   **Sustaining and Expanding Your Practice**

Lifelong Journey: Both writing and Reiki are lifelong practices with endless opportunities for learning and exploration. Staying committed, remaining open to new learning, and engaging with others are essential for maintaining and deepening these practices.

Final Thoughts

Stepping-Stone to Further Growth

This book is a foundation for combining writing and Reiki practices. I encourage you to see this work as a stepping-stone toward more advanced exploration, particularly through structured courses that offer deeper engagement and community interaction.

APPENDIX

BOOKS

"Healing with the Energy of the Chakras" by Cyndi Dale

Offers comprehensive insights into the chakra system and its implications for physical and spiritual health.

"The Artist's Way" by Julia Cameron

A seminal book on creativity that explores the connection between spiritual well-being and creative output.

"The Heart of the Buddha's Teaching" by Thich Nhat Hanh

While not directly related to Reiki, this book provides deep insights into mindfulness and meditation which are complementary to Reiki practices.

"Writing Down the Bones" by Natalie Goldberg

Focuses on freeing the writer within, blending writing theory with Zen wisdom.

REFERENCES

Baikie, K.A., & Wilhelm, K. (2005). Emotional and physical health benefits of expressive writing. *Advances in Psychiatric Treatment*, 11, 338-346.

Baldwin, A.L., & Schwartz, G.E. (2006). Personal interaction with a Reiki practitioner decreases noise-induced microvascular damage in an animal model. *Journal of Alternative and Complementary Medicine.*

Dressen, L. J., & Singg, S. (1998). Effects of Reiki on pain and selected affective and personality variables of chronically ill patients. *Subtle Energies & Energy Medicine Journal Archives.*

King, L.A. (2001). The health benefits of writing about life goals. *Personality and Social Psychology Bulletin*, 27(7), 798-807.

Olson, K., & Hanson, J. (2010). Using Reiki to manage pain: a preliminary report. *Cancer Prevention & Control.*

Pennebaker, J.W., & Beall, S.K. (1986). Confronting a traumatic event: Toward an understanding of inhibition and disease. *Journal of Abnormal Psychology*, 95, 274-281.

Slatcher, R.B., & Pennebaker, J.W. (2006). How do I love thee? Let me count the words: The social effects of expressive writing. *Psychological Science*, 17(8), 660-664.

Smyth, J.M., Stone, A.A., Hurewitz, A., & Kaell, A. (1999). Effects of writing about stressful experiences on symptom reduction in patients with asthma or rheumatoid arthritis: A randomized trial. *JAMA*, 281(14), 1304-1309.

Van der Zee, J., et al. (2019). Effects of Reiki on anxiety and depression in hospital patients: A randomized controlled trial. *Journal of Alternative and Complementary Medicine.*

Vitale, A.T., & O'Connor, P.C. (2006). The effect of Reiki on the quality of life of patients with chronic illnesses. *International Journal of Palliative Nursing.*

RESOURCES

WEBSITES

Reiki.org:

> The International Center for Reiki Training, a useful resource for finding courses, literature, and general information about Reiki practices.

WritersDigest.com:

> Offers writing tips, strategies, and resources for writers at all levels.

NaNoWriMo.org:

> National Novel Writing Month's official site, which provides tools, community, and encouragement for writers attempting to write a novel in a month.

TOOLS AND SOFTWARE

Scrivener:

> A powerful content-generation tool for writers that allows them to structure and manage complex writing projects.

Insight Timer:

> A free app for meditation, important for Reiki practitioners looking to deepen their practice through meditation.

Local Reiki Meetups:

> Listings can be found on Meetup.com for local Reiki sharing groups and circles.

Writing Retreats and Workshops:

> Various options available globally that focus on combining spiritual practices with creative writing, such as those offered by Esalen Institute.

ACKNOWLEDGMENTS

First and foremost, I want to thank my Reiki teacher, Raven Keyes, whose pioneering work in Medical Reiki has been a profound inspiration. Raven's dedication to integrating Reiki into medical settings and her development of the Gold Standards and Best Practices for Medical Reiki have set a remarkable example. Her influence has been instrumental in shaping my approach to combining writing and Reiki. Her books, including "The Healing Power of Reiki" and "Medical Reiki," have provided invaluable insights and have been a constant source of wisdom and encouragement. Raven Keyes passed away on May 3, 2023, in her home in Glastonbury, but her legacy and teachings continue to inspire and guide me (Omega) (RKMRI).

I also extend my heartfelt thanks to Pamela Miles for the invaluable knowledge gained through her Reiki and Medicine Masterclass. Pamela's work in integrating Reiki with conventional medical practices and her contributions to the field have greatly enhanced my understanding and practice of

Reiki in healing. Her course has been pivotal in deepening my skills and confidence as a Reiki practitioner in medical environments.

To my family and friends, your unwavering support and belief in me have been my foundation. Thank you for your love, encouragement, and for always being there as I embarked on this journey.

Finally, to my readers, thank you for your openness and willingness to explore the transformative power of writing and Reiki. I hope this book brings you as much peace and healing as it has brought me in creating it.

ABOUT THE AUTHOR

Nayanda M. Moore is a dedicated writing instructor and Reiki master based in New York City. With over a decade of experience teaching college writing, Nayanda has a deep passion for helping others discover their creative potential and inner peace. She holds a master's degree in Literacy and Language from City College of New York, specializing in andragogy—the methodology and theory of teaching adult learners. Additionally, Nayanda earned a bachelor's degree in Humanities with a concentration in Creative Writing from New York University.

Nayanda's journey began with a love for writing and a deep interest in holistic health. This path led to the discovery of Reiki, a practice that not only complemented her writing but also enhanced her overall well-being. Combining these two passions, Nayanda has developed a method that guides individuals toward personal transformation and self-discovery.

Throughout her career, Nayanda has been passionate about encouraging individuals to find their worth and write

100

their dreams into fruition. She believes in the profound impact of personal storytelling and holistic healing, and her work reflects this philosophy. As the creator of the website, "Write-Your-Life.com," Nayanda offers a supportive space where writers can explore their creativity through courses, workshops, prompts, meditations, and other valuable resources.

When not writing or practicing Reiki, Nayanda enjoys cooking, traveling, kickboxing, and spending time with the people who love her. She is dedicated to facilitating environments where individuals can come together to create, heal, and transform.

"From Pen to Peace: Integrating Writing and Reiki for Transformation" is Nayanda's first book, born out of a desire to share her knowledge and experiences with a broader audience. Through this work, she aims to inspire others to harness the power of writing and Reiki to achieve inner peace and personal fulfillment.

Made in the USA
Middletown, DE
18 September 2024

60581451R00068